Traditional and Healthy Recipes

Corn Dogs from the Linwood Grill

1/2 C. yellow corn meal, finely ground
1/2 C. all-purpose flour
1 T. sugar
1 t. dry mustard (optional)
1 t. baking powder
Pinch salt
1/2 C. milk
1 whole egg, lightly beaten
1 T. melted butter
6 skewers (8 inches each) or popsicle sticks
6 hot dogs
Vegetable oil, for deep frying

Mix the corn meal, flour, sugar, dry mustard, baking powder and salt together in a mixing bowl. Add the milk, beaten egg and melted butter. Mix until smooth.

Using the skewers or popsicle sticks, skewer the hot dogs vertically almost all the way through. Dip each dog in the batter, coating evenly. Be sure not to coat the sticks. (This works best if you pour the mixture into a tall glass).

Deep-fry in vegetable oil at 375 degrees for about 2 minutes until golden brown. Drain on paper towels, let cool for 1 minute and eat!

Makes 6 corn dogs.

Banana Pops

Peel 6 bananas, cut each in half crosswise and insert Popsicle stick in each half. Spread a thin layer of creamy peanut butter over each banana half. Pour a 12-ounce package of chocolate minichips into a small pan or bowl; place bananas in the chips and sprinkle chips to cover all sides. Wrap with wax paper and place in the freezer to harden.

Fajitas-on-a-Stick

1 1/4 lb. boneless beef top sirloin steak, cut 1 inch thick
1/3 C. prepared Italian dressing
3 T. fresh lime juice
2 medium green or red bell peppers, each cut lengthwise into quarters
2 medium onions, each cut crosswise into 1/2 -inch slices
Salt
8 medium flour tortillas, warmed
Prepared salsa
8 9-inch bamboo skewers

Soak eight 9-inch bamboo skewers in enough water to cover for 10 minutes; drain. Trim fat from beef steak. Cut steak crosswise into 1/2-inch-thick strips. Thread an equal amount of beef, weaving back and forth, onto each skewer.

In small bowl, combine dressing and lime juice, mixing well; brush onto beef, peppers, and onions. Place vegetables on grid over medium, ash-covered coals; grill peppers, uncovered, 12 to 15 minutes and onions 15 to 20 minutes or until tender, turning both once.

Approximately 10 minutes before vegetables are done, move vegetables to outer edge of grid. Place beef in center of grid; grill 8 to 10 minutes for medium-rare to medium doneness, turning once.

Season beef with salt, as desired; remove beef from skewers. Serve beef and vegetables in tortillas with salsa.

French Fries

4 or 5 large Russet baking potatoes, 10 to 12 ounces each, about 5 inches long and 2 to 2 1/2 inches across
2 1/2 quarts fresh frying oil
salt

Wash and peel the potatoes, trim into even rectangles and cut into lengthwise slices 3/8-inch wide and swish them in a basin of cold water to remove surface starch.

To prevent discoloration, drain them only just before frying; then dry thoroughly in paper towels.

(May be prepared to this point several hours in advance.)

The first fry: Provide yourself with a bed of paper towels set on a tray. Heat the oil to 325° F. Take up 2 handfuls of the potato strips (about the equivalent of 1 1/2 potatoes) and scatter them into the frying basket. Lower carefully into the hot fat, averting your face to avoid oil sputters. Fry, turning the potatoes frequently for 4 to 5 minutes, or until the potatoes are soft through but not browned. Lift out the basket, let it drain briefly, then spread the potatoes on the paper towels and continue frying remainder. Let cool for 10 minutes or up to 2 to 3 hours.

Second and final frying: Just before serving, heat the frying oil to 375 to 400° F. Fry the cooked potatoes by handfuls, as describe above, turning frequently, only a minute or two, until golden brown. Drain on paper towels, salt lightly, turn the potatoes into a serving basket and continue frying the remainder. Serve as soon as possible.

Makes 6 servings.

Frosty Strawberry Pops

1 pint basket strawberries, stemmed
1 5-oz. can evaporated milk
3 T. frozen orange, cranberry or pineapple juice concentrate
8 wooden craft sticks
8 3-oz. wax-coated paper cups

In blender container, blend strawberries, evaporated milk, and juice concentrate about 1 minute until smooth. Pour into 8 3-ounce, wax-coated paper cups. Place in shallow pan and insert wooden craft stick or plastic spoon into the center of each. Freeze until firm, about 4 hours. After pops are frozen, the can be transferred to a re-sealable plastic bag for freezer storage. To release pops from cups, dip briefly into hot water up to rim of cup.

Yield: 8 servings

Berry Banana Fruit Smoothies

1 medium ripe banana
1 container (8 oz.) raspberry or strawberry yogurt
1 can (6 oz.) unsweetened pineapple juice (3/4 C.)

Peel banana. Cut banana into 2-inch pieces. Slice banana and place in Quick-Stir Pitcher. Mash banana until fairly smooth.

Add yogurt and juice to pitcher. Mix well. Pour into drinking classes.

Funnel Cakes

3 large eggs
2 1/4 C. milk
1/2 t. pure lemon extract
4 C. flour
1 C. light brown sugar
1 T. baking powder
1/2 t. salt
Oil for frying
Cinnamon powdered sugar for dusting

Preheat the oil to 375 degrees F.

In a mixing bowl, whisk the eggs, milk, and lemon. Whisk well. Sift the flour, sugar, baking powder, and salt together. Fold the flour mixture into the egg mixture. Stir until smooth.

Hold your finger over the funnel opening, fill with 3/4 cup of the filling. Place your hand over the oil and carefully remove your finger. Scribble and crisscross the filling into the hot oil.

Fry until golden on both sides. Remove from the oil and drain on paper towels. Dust with cinnamon sugar mix. Repeat the process until all of the batter is used.

Italian Sausages with Peppers and Onions

1 1/2 pounds Italian sausage
2 green peppers, sliced
1/2 cup water
2 onions, sliced
2 tablespoons olive oil
2 long hard rolls

Place sausage in hot cast iron skillet and brown on all sides. Add water, cover and let steam for 5 to 8 minutes or until sausages are no longer pink in the middle. Remove to plate. Drain off any remaining water from skillet.

Add olive oil to same skillet along with peppers and onions. Cook over medium heat until soft, about 20 minutes. Place sausage in a roll with peppers and onions. Serve.

Cockleburs

1 C. sugar
1/2 C. water
10 oz. pkg. raw peanuts
1/2 t. salt
1/4 t. red food coloring, optional

Boil sugar and water until sugar is completely dissolved. Add food coloring if desired.

Add peanuts. Cook until most of the moisture is absorbed, stirring constantly.

Pour onto a greased jelly roll pan. Bake 325 degrees for 10 minutes. Stir. Sprinkle with salt. Return to oven.

Bake 20 minutes more. Remove and cool.

Candied Apples

2 C. granulated sugar
2 C. corn syrup
1/3 C. cinnamon candy
1 C. water
3/4 t. cinnamon
1/2 t. vanilla
1/4 t. cloves
3/4 t. red food coloring
6 apples

Remove stems from apples, wash, and pat dry. Insert a wooden skewer in each apple, running through the apple from stem end to base without protruding all the way through the bottom end.

Combine sugar, corn syrup, cinnamon candies, and water in medium-sized saucepan. Cook until candies dissolve, stirring constantly. Be careful not to boil. Add cinnamon, vanilla, cloves, and food coloring. Mix thoroughly. Boil mixture to 300° F. using a candy thermometer without stirring.

While mixture is boiling, generously prepare a baking sheet with cooking spray so it's ready ahead of time. As soon as mixture reaches 300° F., remove it from heat and quickly dip each apple-one by one-into the mixture until it is thoroughly coated.

Set coated apples, standing on their bottoms with skewer pointing up, on baking sheet until mixture hardens. Let apples reach room temperature before eating.

Navajo Fry Bread

3 C. unbleached white flour
1 C. masa corn flour (not cornmeal)
3 T. sugar
1/2 t. salt
2 t. baking powder
1 C. warm water
Peanut oil or lard for deep-frying

You will need a wok or deep heavy pot for deep-frying, a medium-sized bowl and tongs.

Fill your wok or pan with 2 inches of peanut oil or lard and heat over medium to medium-high heat.

Meanwhile, combine the dry ingredients in a bowl. Make a well in the center and stir in the water. Mix to form a dough, and knead briefly. The dough should be soft but not sticky. Add a little more flour or water if necessary.

Cut the dough into 8 equal pieces. Flatten one piece to a thin disc about 5 inches in diameter and less than 1/4inch thick. Cut a 1-inch triangular wedge out of the center of the bread and test the oil temperature by dropping the wedge into the oil. The oil should sizzle quietly and the dough wedge should begin to change color. If it burns or sizzles fiercely, the temperature is too high; adjust it accordingly. Slide the bread into the oil (the oil will sizzle and bubble up through the hole in the middle) and cook until golden on the bottom, about 2 to 3 minutes.

Then turn over, taking care not to splash yourself with oil, and cook until golden, approximately 1 1/2to 2 1/2more minutes. As the bread cooks, shape the next one and cut a triangular hole in the center.

Place the cooked bread on a plate lined with paper towels to drain while you prepare and cook the remaining breads. Serve warm.

Makes 8 servings

Indian Fry-bread Tacos

Fry bread mix:

4 C. white flour
1/2 t. salt
1 T. baking powder
1 3/4 C. lukewarm water

Indian taco toppings:

1 22-oz. can of chili beans (or make your own pot of beans)
4 large ripe tomatoes
1 head of lettuce
2 lbs. hamburger
1 lb. cheddar cheese

Fry bread:

Combine all dry ingredients. Add water and knead until dough is soft but not sticky. Add more flour if needed. Let dough sit for 4 hours and knead occasionally. Shape dough into balls the size of a small apple. Roll out dough to the size of a tortilla. Dough should be about 1/2-inch thick. Poke a small hole in the middle. Fry dough mixture in hot vegetable oil; oil should be about an inch deep. Brown on both sides. Drain and serve hot. (A shortcut for flour mixture is Gold Medal Self-Rising Flour and water; 4 cups self-rising flour and 2 cups lukewarm water.)

Indian taco toppings:

Cook hamburger and season to your taste. Prepare beans. Dice tomatoes, chop cheese, shred lettuce. Spread meat and bean mixture on hot bread, top with lettuce, tomatoes and cheese.

Chicken Fried Oyster Tacos

16 oysters, shucked
1/2 C. buttermilk
1/2 C. white cornmeal
1/2 t. salt
1/2 t. pepper
Canola oil, for frying
2/3 C. sour cream
2 chipotle peppers in adobo sauce, chopped
1 T. fresh lime juice
2 T. chopped garlic
Salt, to taste 8 heated corn tortillas (can substitute flour)
1 head Boston lettuce, rinsed, drained and torn
1 C. diced, seeded tomatoes

Soak oysters in buttermilk for 5 minutes. Place cornmeal, salt and pepper in flat bowl and dredge oysters in mixture and set on plate to fry.

In small skillet, pour canola oil to 1 inch depth and heat to 375 degrees. When oil is hot, slip in the oysters and cook 1 minute. Transfer to paper towels and keep warm while others are being fried.

To make the sauce, combine sour cream, chopped chipotle, lime juice, garlic and salt. Cover and place in refrigerator until ready to serve.

To serve, place 2 oysters on each tortilla, top with lettuce, tomatoes and chipotle sour cream sauce.

Makes 8 appetizer servings.

STATE FAIR CAKE

1 1/2 c. sugar
1/2 c. butter
2 eggs
1 c. water, or half milk and half water
2 1/4 c. flour
2 tsp. baking powder
Salt

Cream sugar and butter. Add eggs and beat until white or light in color (this is the secret to this cake). Mix flour and baking powder and add alternately with liquid.

FOR SPICE CAKE, ADD:

1/2 tsp. cloves
1 tsp. cinnamon
1 tsp. nutmeg

FOR MARBLE CAKE, TAKE HALF OF MIXTURE AND ADD:

1 sq. chocolate
1 tsp. cloves
1/2 tsp. cinnamon
1/2 tsp. nutmeg

Or use half of mixture and add red food coloring.

AMBER'S COUNTY FAIR MUFFINS

1 3/4 c. unsifted all-purpose flour
2 tbsp. sugar
2 1/2 tsp. baking powder
1/2 tsp. salt
1 egg, well beaten
3/4 c. milk
1/3 c. liquid shortening

Preheat oven to 400 degrees. Grease muffin pan. Combine flour, sugar, baking powder and salt in large bowl. Stir well. Combine egg and milk in small bowl, the pour into the dry ingredients. Add shortening. Stir just until moist. (Batter will be lumpy.)

Spoon into greased muffin pan, filling each about 2/3 full. Bake until golden brown. (Delicious served warm with jelly or honey!)

ANTIQUE FAIR BEEF BARBECUE

1 (3 - 3 1/2 lb.) chuck roast 1 can consomme

Put roast in Dutch oven, add consomme. Do not brown roast. Simmer 5 to 6 hours, covered, until meat pulls apart easily. If necessary, add more consomme during cooking. Remove meat, skin excess grease from consomme (easier if cooled first), and measure remaining liquid for use in the following sauce.

SAUCE:

1 lg. onion, sliced very thin
1 c. chopped celery
1/4 c. brown sugar
1/4 c. prepared mustard
2 tbsp. Worcestershire sauce
2 c. reserved liquid, adding water if needed
1 c. catsup
1 (15 oz.) can tomato sauce

Cook onion and celery in small amount of oil until tender. Add remaining ingredients. Simmer 20 minutes. Shred roast (easier if cool) and add to sauce. If it becomes too thick, dilute with consomme, water or tomato juice. Will fill 12 to 14 buns; serves about 8.

CHERYL'S COUNTY FAIR ZUCCHINI BREAD

3 eggs
1 c. oil
1 1/2 c. sugar
1 tsp. salt
3 tsp. cinnamon
2 tbsp. grated orange peel
2 c. grated zucchini
3 tsp. vanilla
3 c. flour
1 tsp. soda
1/4 tsp. baking powder
1 c. chopped walnuts

Beat egg yolks until light and fluffy. Add the oil, sugar, salt, cinnamon, orange peel, zucchini and vanilla. Mix well.

Combine the flour, soda, baking powder and walnuts and add to above mixture. Bake at 325 degrees for 1 hour. Makes 2 loaves.

CHICKEN SCARBOUROUGH FAIR

3 chicken breasts, boned, skinned and halved
1/2 c. butter, melted
Salt, pepper
6 slices Mozzarella cheese
Flour
1 egg, beaten
Fine dry bread crumbs
2 tbsp. chopped parsley
1/4 tsp. sage
1/4 tsp. rosemary
1/4 tsp. thyme
1/2 c. dry white wine

Flatten chicken between sheets of wax paper. Spread flattened breasts with half the butter. Season with salt and pepper and place 1 slice cheese on top of each. Roll chicken, tucking in ends. Coat lightly with flour. Dip in beaten egg. Roll in bread crumbs.

Arrange chicken rolls, seam side down, in shallow baking dish. Refrigerate at this point if not baking immediately. Before serving, remove dish from refrigerator. Melt remaining butter and add parsley, sage, rosemary and thyme. Bake at 350 degrees for 30 minutes basting with butter mixture. Pour in wine and bake and additional 20 minutes, basting with pan liquid. Serve chicken rolls on platter or individual plates and spoon pan liquid around rolls. Makes 6 servings. You may want to add garlic or shallots.

COUNTRY FAIR BREAD

3 pkg. dry yeast
1/3 c. honey
2 eggs, beaten
1 c. dry milk
2 c. whole wheat flour
4 1/2 c. warm water
1/4 c. melted shortening
12-14 c. flour
1 c. rye flour

Preheat oven to 400 degrees. Dissolve yeast in water; add honey and eggs. In large bowl mix dry milk, salt and 4 cups of flour (for whole wheat bread, substitute whole wheat and rye flour for 3 cups). Add yeast mixture and mix well. Add shortening and let stand until bubbles form (20 minutes). Add flour, 1 cup at a time until stiff.

Turn on floured board and knead until elastic. Let rise in greased bowl until double. Form into 4 loaves. Let rise to 1 1/2 inches above pan. Bake at 400 degrees for 15 minutes; reduce to 375 degrees and bake 20 minutes. Loaves should sound hollow. Cool on rack before wrapping. Freezes well. Makes 4 loaves.

Notes: Begin with whole wheat and rye flour for whole wheat bread. Bon Apetit!

1 1/2 c. cooked brown rice
1 (10 1/2 oz.) can cream of chicken soup
1 c. diced cheddar cheese
1/2 c. half and half
2 (10 oz.) pkgs. frozen broccoli

Cook broccoli; drain well. Mix other ingredients well. Layer alternately with broccoli in 1 1/2 quart casserole. Cover and bake in 350 degree oven for 25 to 30 minutes.

1 (8 oz.) pkg. elbow macaroni 1 lb. ground beef
1 c. chopped onion
1 tsp. salt
1/4 tsp. pepper
1 can cream of celery soup 1 (8 oz.) carton sour cream 1 can English peas, drained

Cook macaroni according to package directions; drain. Combine ground beef, onion and seasonings in a skillet. Saute meat mixture until lightly browned; drain. Stir in cream of celery soup; cover and simmer 10 minutes. Stir in macaroni and remaining ingredients; bake in lightly greased 2 1/2 or 3 quart casserole dish for 35 minutes at 350 degrees. Serves 8.

COUNTRY FAIR CHICKEN

2 1/2 - 3 lb. cut up fryer
1/2 c. Parmesan cheese
1/4 c. flour
1 tsp. paprika
Dash of pepper
1 slightly beaten egg
1 tbsp. milk
1/4 tsp. butter

Combine cheese, flour and seasonings. Dip chicken in combination of egg and milk. Coat with cheese mixture. Place in baking dish. Pour melted butter over chicken. Bake at 350 degrees for 1 hour

COUNTRY FAIR PORK CHOPS

2/3 c. Worcestershire sauce
1/2 c. vegetable oil
1/2 c. cider vinegar
1/4. water
8 pork chops, 1 inch thick, center cut best

In spray bottle, mix Worcestershire sauce, oil, cider and water. Makes 7/8 cup. Spray chops on both sides with mixture. Grill chops about 4 inches from heat on first side about 10 minutes. Turn, spray again with mixture and grill on second side 10 minutes. Spray several times while cooking.

Note: Mixture, if desired, can be used to marinate pork chops several hours in refrigerator before grilling.

COUNTY FAIR AWARD WINNING ZUCCHINI CAKE

1/2 c. butter
1/2 c. oil (vegetable)
1 3/4 c. sugar
2 eggs
1 tsp. vanilla
1/2 c. buttermilk OR 1/2 c. milk + 1 tsp. vinegar
2 1/2 c. flour
1/4 c. cocoa
1 tsp. soda
1 tsp. baking powder
1/2 tsp. salt
1/2 tsp. cinnamon
1/4 c. chopped nuts (optional)
2 c. grated zucchini
1/2 c. chocolate chips

Mix butter, oil and sugar. Add eggs and mix. Add vanilla and buttermilk. Stir in flour, cocoa, soda, baking powder, salt, cinnamon. Mix well. Add zucchini and nuts. Mix thoroughly. Pour into 13 x 9 inch pan. Sprinkle chocolate chips on top before baking. Bake at 325 degrees for 40-45 minutes.

COUNTY FAIR BAKED BEANS

1 (28 oz.) can Campbell's pork and beans
1/4 c. catsup
1/4 c. brown sugar
1 tbsp. finely chopped onion
1 tsp. prepared mustard

Combine all ingredients in 1-quart casserole. Bake at 350 degrees for 1 hour.

2 1/2 lb. boneless beef, trimmed
2 1/2 lb. boneless pork shoulder, trimmed
2 qt. water
2 ribs celery, cut up lg.
2 carrots, cut up lg.
2 sm. bay leaves
8 whole cloves
1 tsp. salt
1/4 tsp. black pepper

SAUCE;

2 tbsp. butter
1 c. chopped onion
1 1/2 c. water
1 c. catsup
1/2 c. cider vinegar
1/3 c. sugar
1 tbsp. plus 1 tsp. Worcestershire
1 tbsp. brown sugar
2 tsp. celery salt
2 tsp. paprika
1/2 tsp. ground cumin
1/2 tsp. black pepper
1/2 tsp. salt

MEAT: Preheat oven to 325 degrees. Place meat, vegetables, and seasonings in large roaster. Cover and bake for 3 hours. Remove pork and continue cooking beef for another hour or until tender. Remove meat and shred into bite size pieces while warm using 2 forks. Reserve broth for another use.

SAUCE: In large saucepan, saute onion and butter until onion is transparent. Add remaining ingredients and mix well. Add shredded meats, simmer over low heat until mixture is thick and juice, about 15 minutes. Do NOT stir too often - meat should stay in good size pieces. Serve hot 2 1/2 lb. boneless beef, trimmed

2 1/2 lb. boneless pork shoulder, trimmed 2 qt. water
2 ribs celery, cut up lg.

2 carrots, cut up lg.
2 sm. bay leaves
8 whole cloves
1 tsp. salt
1/4 tsp. black pepper

SAUCE;

2 tbsp. butter
1 c. chopped onion
1 1/2 c. water
1 c. catsup
1/2 c. cider vinegar
1/3 c. sugar
1 tbsp. plus 1 tsp. Worcestershire
1 tbsp. brown sugar
2 tsp. celery salt
2 tsp. paprika
1/2 tsp. ground cumin
1/2 tsp. black pepper
1/2 tsp. salt

MEAT: Preheat oven to 325 degrees. Place meat, vegetables, and seasonings in large roaster. Cover and bake for 3 hours. Remove pork and continue cooking beef for another hour or until tender. Remove meat and shred into bite size pieces while warm using 2 forks. Reserve broth for another use.

SAUCE: In large saucepan, saute onion and butter until onion is transparent. Add remaining ingredients and mix well. Add shredded meats, simmer over low heat until mixture is thick and juice, about 15 minutes. Do NOT stir too often - meat should stay in good size pieces. Serve hot

COUNTY FAIR BREAD

5 to 5 1/2 c. all-purpose flour
1/4 c. sugar
2 tsp. salt
1 pkg. active dry yeast
1 1/2 c. milk
1/4 c. shortening
2 eggs
1 tbsp. water
1 egg white, slightly beaten Poppy seeds or sesame seeds

In large mixer bowl, combine 2 cups flour, sugar, salt, and dry yeast. In saucepan, heat milk and shortening until milk is warm (shortening does not need to melt). Add eggs and warm milk to flour mixture. Blend at lowest speed until moistened; beat 3 minutes at medium speed. By hand, stir in remaining flour to form a stiff dough. Knead on floured surface until smooth and elastic, about 3 minutes. Place in greased bowl, turning to grease top.

Cover; let rise in warm place until light and doubled in size, 1 1/2 hours. Punch down dough; divide into 6 portions. Shape each portion into a strip 8 inches long by rolling between hands. Braid three strips together. Place braid on greased cookie sheet. Braid remaining three strips and place on cookie sheet. Cover; let rise in warm place until light and doubled in size, about 45 minutes. Brush with mixture of egg white and water. Sprinkle with poppy seeds or sesame seeds. Bake at 375 degrees for 35-40 minutes until golden brown

COUNTY FAIR CARROT CAKE

1 1/2 c. oil
2 c. sugar
4 eggs, separated
3 c. carrots, grated
2 c. flour
2 tsp. cinnamon
2 tsp. baking soda
1 tsp. salt

ICING:

2 c. powdered sugar
2 tsp. vanilla
8 oz. cream cheese

Blend together oil and sugar. Add egg yolks and blend. Stir in carrots. Add flour, cinnamon, soda and salt and mix. Fold in beaten egg whites. Pour batter into greased and floured 9"x13" cake pan. Bake at 350 degrees for 30 to 35 minutes.

TO make icing blend sugar with softened cream cheese. Add vanilla and mix on high until smooth and creamy.

COUNTY FAIR CHAMPION GINGER SNAP COOKIES

3/4 c. shortening
1 c. sugar
1/4 c. molasses
1 egg
2 c. flour
2 tsp. soda
1/4 tsp. salt
1 tsp. cinnamon
1 tsp. cloves
1 tsp. ginger

Cream shortening and sugar. Add molasses and egg, beat. Add dry ingredients, mix well. Roll in small balls, dip into sugar. Bake at 375 degrees, for 12-15 minutes on greased sheet.

COUNTY FAIR CASSEROLE

6-8 potatoes
1 green pepper
1 lg. onion
2 lbs. roasted sausage
1 1/2-2 c. milk
Velveeta cheese

Peel and slice potatoes into large greased casserole dish. Alternate with green pepper and onion. Cut roasted sausage into 1 inch pieces and place on top. Cover with slices of Velveeta cheese, enough to cover top of dish. Add milk. Bake 1 1/2 to 2 hours at 350 degrees.

COUNTY FAIR CHERRY COFFEE CAKE

4 eggs
1 c. white sugar
1 c. oil
2 c. flour
1 tsp. baking powder
1/2 tsp. salt
1 can cherry pie filling

Mix all ingredients together except pie filling. Pour half the batter into greased 9x13 inch pan. Spread pie filling on batter. Pour remaining batter (ribbon fashion) on top of pie filling. Sprinkle cinnamon on top. Bake for 35 minutes at 350 degrees.

May be a little longer. Make sure middle is set. Drizzle confectioners' glaze over while still warm.

COUNTY FAIR CHICKEN

1/2 c. (2 oz.) grated Parmesan cheese
1/4 c. flour
1 tsp. paprika - 1/2 tsp. salt - dash of pepper
2 1/2 to 3 lbs. fryer chicken, cutup
1 egg, slightly beaten
1 tbsp. milk
1/4 c. melted butter

Combine cheese, flour and seasonings. Dip chicken in combined egg and milk. Coat with cheese mixture. Place in 8 x 12 inch baking dish. Pour butter over chicken. Bake at 350 degrees for 1 hour

COUNTY FAIR ELEPHANT EARS

1 1/2 c. milk
1 tsp. salt
2 packets dry yeast
2 tbsp. sugar
6 tbsp. shortening
4 c. flour
Oil for frying
Powdered sugar, sifted Cinnamon/sugar mix

Heat but do not boil milk, sugar, salt and shortening until shortening is melted. Cool to lukewarm. Add yeast and stir until dissolved. Stir in flour 2 cups at a time, beating until smooth after reach addition.

Put into greased bowl. Cover with damp cloth, let rise until double. Dust hands with flour. Pinch off pieces of dough size of golf ball. Stretch into 6-8 inch circle. Drop into hot oil in pan large enough to fry 6-8 pieces. Fry until pieces rise, turn with tongs and fry until light brown. Drain on paper towels and sprinkle with desired topping.

COUNTY FAIR ICE CREAM

2 c. sugar
6 tbsp. flour
1 tsp. salt
5 c. milk
6 eggs
4 c. Half and Half
3 tbsp. vanilla extract About 20 lbs. ice
2 to 3 c. rock salt

In large saucepan combine sugar, flour and salt. In medium bowl beat milk and eggs. Add to sugar mixture and blend. Cook over low heat, stirring constantly until mixture thickens and coats spoon, about 30 minutes. Cover and refrigerate to cool about 2 hours.

Pour mixture, Half and Half and vanilla into 4 to 6 quart ice cream freezer can. Add dasher, cover and place in freezer bucket. Half fill bucket with ice, sprinkle with salt. Alternate layers of ice and salt until about 1 inch below can lid.

Turn crank and freeze until stiff. It will take 35-45 minutes. Ice cream will be soft. Remove dasher, pack down ice cream and allow to harden. Makes 3 quarts.

COUNTY FAIR PANCAKES

1 qt. med. sour buttermilk
3 eggs
1 tsp. salt
1 tbsp. sugar
4 tbsp. melted fat
1 tsp. baking powder and 1 tsp. soda sifted with enough flour to make a medium batter

Beat eggs separately and fold in whites last

COUNTY FAIR PEACH PIE

3 c. presifted all-purpose flour
1 tsp. iodized salt
1 c. vegetable shortening
1 egg
1/4 c. cold water
1 tbsp. vinegar

PEACH FILLING:

2 cans (1 lb. 13 oz. each) sliced peaches
2/3 c. sugar
1/4 c. cornstarch

Dash salt

2 1/2 tbsp. butter
1 tbsp. lemon juice

Make crust: Combine flour and salt. Cut in shortening. Beat egg and add water and vinegar; add to dry mixture a tablespoon at a time and toss to mix. Divide in two uneven halves and roll out larger half on lightly floured board, 1/8 inch thick. Line a 10 inch pie pan.

Preheat oven to 400 degrees.

Make filling: Drain peaches, reserving 1/2 cup syrup. In saucepan, combine sugar, cornstarch and salt; stir in syrup. Cook and stir until thick and clear. Add butter and lemon juice, then peaches. Pour into crust.

Roll out remaining pastry. Cut shapes in top crust with small cutter. Roll crust up on rolling pin and unroll on top of pie. Seal and crimp edges.

Bake in 400 degree oven for 40 to 45 minutes. Plan to eat warm. This pie takes literally hours like five - to cool.

COUNTY FAIR SPUDS

1 pkg. (8 serving size) instant mashed potatoes
1 pkg. (8 oz.) cream cheese, softened
1/3 c. chopped onion
1 egg (beaten)
Salt and pepper to taste

Prepare mashed potatoes according to package directions, reducing water to 2 1/4 cups and omitting salt. Blend cream cheese into hot mashed potatoes. Add onion, egg, salt and pepper; mix well. Transfer to a lightly greased 1 1/2 quart casserole dish. Bake in a preheated 350 degree oven for 45 minutes.

Note: This dish freezes well, so it can be assembled and frozen before baking. Let thaw in refrigerator before baking

FAIR KITCHEN MEATLOAF

10 lb. ground beef
2 c. chopped onion
10 eggs
10 c. cracker crumbs
6 c. tomato juice (46 oz. can)
10 tsp. salt
4 tsp. pepper

Mix all together and bake about 2 hours at 350 degrees in two 9 x 13 inch pans.

FAIR LEMON PIE

1 c. sugar
1/4 c. cornstarch
1/4 tsp. salt
1 1/2 c. water
3 egg yolks
2 tbsp. butter
1/3 c. lemon juice
1 1/2 tsp. grated lemon rind

MERINGUE:

3 egg whites 6 tbsp. sugar

FOR PIE: Combine 1/2 cup sugar, cornstarch and salt in double boiler, gradually blend in water and stir constantly until thickened. Beat together egg yolks, 1/2 cup sugar and a little hot mixture; then stir all into remaining hot mixture. Cook over double boiler 2 minutes, stirring constantly. Remove and add butter, lemon juice and lemon rind. Cool and pour into 9 inch baked pie shell. MERINGUE: Beat egg whites until foamy. Add sugar, 1 tablespoon at a time, beating after each addition until stiff. Spread over top of pie. Sprinkle shredded coconut over top and bake at 425 degrees for 5 minutes.

FAIR POTATOES

1 egg, beaten
2 c. milk
1 c. grated Swiss cheese
1 to 2 tsp. salt
1/4 tsp. freshly ground pepper
Dash of freshly ground nutmeg
Garlic powder to taste
5 c. coarsely grated potatoes (about 4 bakers)
2 tbsp. butter

Mix beaten egg, milk, seasonings and 3/4 cup of the cheese. Mix well with the potatoes and pour into a well buttered 1 1/2 quart casserole. Cut 1 tablespoon of the butter in small pieces and push into the potatoes. Cut the other tablespoon of butter in pieces and distribute over the top. Sprinkle with remaining 1/4 cup cheese. Bake at 350 degrees for 1 hour and fifteen minutes. The original recipe called for 2 teaspoons but the church volunteers cut the amount. Try 1/8 teaspoon garlic powder the first time.

FAIR SOFT TACOS

1 lb. ground beef
1-3 cloves garlic, minced
Salt
Pepper
3 or 4 green onion, minced
3/4 c. chopped lettuce
12 corn tortillas
Oil
Taco sauce
1/2 c. coarsely mashed potatoes (with milk and butter)

In skillet, slowly cook beef until browned. Add garlic, salt and pepper to taste. Drain fat. Add green onions, lettuce, mashed potatoes, and taco sauce to taste. Simmer slowly, about 7 minutes. In hot oil, heat tortillas, one at a time, just until softened. Blot dry with paper towels. Put spoonful of meat mixture on tortilla and roll up.

FOOD FAIR KING RANCH CHICKEN

Tortilla chips, broken
1 chicken, simmered, boned & shredded
1 can cream of mushroom soup with a lg. chunk of Velveeta melted in it
1 can cream of chicken soup
1 can Ro-tel tomatoes
1 can green chilies
1/2 c. chicken stock
1/2 - 1 c. onions, chopped

Enough grated Cheddar cheese to cover casserole

Layer the casserole in tortilla chips (tortillas may be substituted), then a layer of chicken. Make a sauce by combining the soups, tomatoes, chiles (can omit for a very mild version), and the chicken stock. Mix well and pour over chicken. Next, a layer of chopped onions is sprinkled over the sauce, then a generous layer of grated Cheddar cheese. This recipe will fill 1 large casserole or 2 small (cake pan size) ones.

FUN FAIR BROWNIE PIZZA

1 lg. box brownie mix
2 eggs
1/3 c. water
1/4 c. oil
1 c. chopped mini peanut butter cups
1 c. mini marshmallows
1 c. candy coated pieces

Preheat oven to 350 degrees. Grease a 10 to 11 inch pizza pan. Stir together mix, eggs, water and oil in large bowl (about 50 strokes). Spread mix in pan.

Bake at 350 degrees for 20-25 minutes, or until brownie begins to pull away from the edge of pan. Remove from oven; sprinkle peanut butter cups and marshmallows evenly over top. Return to oven and bake 5 minutes or until marshmallows begin to puff. Remove; add rest of candy on top. Cool completely before serving.

HARVEST FAIR CHILI

5 lbs. red beans
1/2 bushel tomatoes, chopped
10 hot peppers, chopped
6 lg. eggplants, peeled and cut in 1 inch cubes
5 sweet peppers, chopped
10 onions, chopped finely
2 lg. cans tomato puree
1/4 c. chili powder
1/2 c. oil

Pick over beans to clean of small rocks. Rinse and cover well with water. Bring to boil turn off heat and let sit 2 to 3 hours. Rinse and cover with fresh water. Bring to boil, let simmer 1 1/2 hours until beans are tender.

Saute onions and eggplant until translucent, add peppers hot and sweet and saute 5 minutes. Add tomatoes and puree. Cook another 20 minutes and then add cooked beans and chili powder. Serve with corn chips, grated cheese and fresh salsa.

JOHNNY KAW FAIR SLOPPY JOES

5 lbs. hamburger
1 pt. tomatoes
1 pt. tomato sauce
1/3 pt. catsup
1 sm. onion, peeled
1/2 green pepper, seeded
2 tsp. salt
2 tbsp. sugar

Brown hamburger and drain fat. Blend remaining ingredients until liquid. Pour into hamburger and simmer 30 minutes. This is a large quantity, approximately 1/2 gallon of Sloppy Joe Mix.

KENTUCKY STATE FAIR FAVORITE CAKE

1 1/2 c. plus 2 tbsp. sugar
2 c. flour
2 1/2 tsp. cinnamon
1 (4 oz.) shredded coconut
1 (8 oz.) can crushed pineapple
1 tsp. baking soda
1 1/4 c. oil
1/2 tsp. salt
4 eggs

Combine all ingredients in a large bowl. Blend with electric mixer at low speed until ingredients are combined. Turn mixer to medium speed; beat until smooth. Pour in greased and floured pan. Bake about 45 minutes in preheated 350 degree oven. Use a cake pan that has lid for storage.

ICING:

2/3 stick butter
1 lb. powdered sugar
1 c. chopped pecans (or other nuts)
1 (8 oz.) cream cheese
2 tsp. vanilla

Whip butter and cream cheese together. Add other ingredients and beat well.

KID'S FAIR SUGAR COOKIES

2/3 c. shortening
3/4 c. granulated sugar
1 tsp. vanilla
1 egg
4 tsp. milk
2 c. sifted flour
1 1/2 tsp. baking powder
1/4 tsp. salt

Thoroughly cream shortening, sugar and vanilla. Add egg and milk. Beat until light and fluffy. Sift together dry ingredients, blend into creamed mixture. Cover and chill for 1 hour at least. On lightly floured surface, roll to 1/8" thickness. Use tuna can to cut. Bake on ungreased cookie sheet at 375 degrees for about 8 to 10 minutes.

MICHIGAN FAIR COOKIES

Cream: 2 c. brown sugar 2 eggs

Mix with: 2 c. oatmeal 1 tsp. baking powder 1 tsp. baking soda 1/2 tsp. salt 1 tsp. vanilla

Add: 1 c. chocolate chips

Chill in refrigerator 1 hour. Make in balls about walnut size, then roll in confectioners' sugar. Then bake at 375 degrees for about 8 minutes.

MOM'S COUNTY FAIR SWEEPSTAKES WINNING LEMON MERINGUE PIE

1 baked pie shell

FILLING:

1 1/2 c. sugar
1/3 c. cornstarch
1/4 tsp. salt
4 egg yolks
2 tbsp. grated lemon peel
2 tbsp. butter
1/4 c. lemon juice

In heavy 2-quart saucepan, combine sugar, cornstarch, and salt. Gradually stir in 1 1/2 cups water. Over medium heat, bring to boil, stirring constantly. Boil 1 minute. Mixture will become thick and translucent. Remove from heat.

Stir a little of mixture into egg yolks, continue adding mixture until equal parts. Pour all back into mixture. Stir and add grated lemon. Stir constantly over medium heat until mixture boils again. Boil 1 minute, remove from heat. Add butter. Stir until melted. Gradually add lemon juice. Pour into center of pie shell. Fill will spread out evenly by itself. Let cool while making meringue.

MERINGUE:

2/3 c. egg whites (4 lg.)
1/4 tsp. salt
1/4 tsp. cream of tartar
1/2 c. sugar

Have egg whites at room temperature in medium bowl. Preheat oven to 375 degrees. With mixer at high speed, beat egg whites just until foamy throughout. Add salt and cream of tartar. Beat just to blend well. Add sugar slowly. Beat until meringue is shiny and stiff peaks form. Spread meringue on pie. Make sure to seal edges. Bake 12 to 15 minutes until lightly brown.

MORE THAN A FAIR SHAKE

May be a breakfast in itself or a mid-morning or afternoon refresher, has several advantages over a milkshake. It is lower in calories and can be even lower if low-fat milk and lowfat yogurt are used. 1 c. plain yogurt (lowfat or nonfat, as desired) 10 oz. pkg. frozen fruit (strawberries, peaches, blueberries, raspberries) Sugar or artificial sweetener, optional

Place milk, yogurt, and frozen fruit in an electric blender container. If the fruit is unsweetened. You may want to add sugar or artificial sweetener to taste. Cover and process until smooth. Yield 1 serving.

MRS. MINNIE'S RAISIN PIE (USED FOR THE FAIR)

3 eggs
3/4 c. light brown sugar
1/4 c. soft butter
1 c. Karo molasses (Blue label)
1/4 c. black walnuts (crushed)
1 c. raisins
1 tsp. vanilla

Beat eggs adding sugar and butter beating at all times until thick and fluffy. Beat in molasses until that is fluffy. Add walnuts and vanilla, beat gently while adding raisins. Pour into unbaked pie shell. Bake at 375 degrees for 30 minutes or just firm in center. Makes 1 (9 inch) pie.

NESHOBA COUNTY FAIR CASSEROLE

1 fryer
1 pkg. vermicelli spaghetti (approx. 8 oz.)
1/2 to 1 lb. hoop or sharp cheese, grated
1 lg. bell pepper, chopped
1 lg. onion, chopped
1 can sm. English peas
1 can Rotel tomatoes
Salt & pepper
1 stick butter

Boil fryer and take off bone. Cook spaghetti in chicken broth. Add cheese. Cook onion and pepper in butter until soft and add to spaghetti. Add peas and Rotel tomatoes. Salt and pepper to taste. Place in buttered casserole dish and bake 45 minutes to 1 hour.

PARTY FAIR MEAT BALLS

1 lb. lean ground beef
1 egg
1 tbsp. cornstarch
3/4 c. finely chopped onions Salt and pepper to taste Cooking oil

Combine these ingredients and form into very small balls. Fry in oil and then drain. In another pan, heat 1 cup of pineapple juice with 1 tablespoon of oil and add the following ingredients that have been mixed together:

1/2 c. sugar
3 tbsp. cornstarch
1 tbsp. soy sauce
3 tbsp. vinegar
6 tbsp. water

Cook this mixture, stirring constantly until it thickens. Then add the meatballs. Can add 1 (8 1/2 oz.) drained pineapple bits and 1 large green sweet pepper, cut in strips. (If preferred, omit pepper.) Bring all this just to the point where it is good and hot, but do not cook or the color and crispness of the pepper will be lost.

PRIZE WINNING BROWNIES

2 sticks butter
2 c. sugar
1 tsp. vanilla
1 c. flour
2/3 c. unsweetened cocoa
2 c. walnuts
4 eggs
1/2 tsp. baking powder

Mix all ingredients thoroughly. Grease a square pan. Pour batter into pan. Bake at 350 degrees for 30 minutes.

SCARBOROUGH FAIR SALAD

1 lb. Louis Rich breast of turkey (any variety)
1 pkg. (2 oz.) slivered almonds
1 tart apple
1 tsp. lemon juice
2 stalks celery, chopped
2 green onions with tops, chopped
1 tbsp. chopped fresh parsley

Cut turkey into 1/2 inch cubes; set aside. Toast almonds in shallow baking pan in 350 degree oven for 8 minutes or until lightly browned, cool. Cut apple into chunks and toss with lemon juice in large bowl, add turkey, almonds, celery, onion and parsley.

HERB DRESSING:

1/2 c. mayonnaise
1/4 tsp. ground thyme
1/2 tsp. garlic powder
1/2 tsp. oregano leaves
1/2 tsp. pepper
1/2 tsp. rosemary leaves
1/2 tsp. sage

Combine dressing ingredients in small bowl; add to turkey mixture and toss. Cover and chill thoroughly. Makes 4 (1 1/2 cups) servings.

STATE FAIR CARAMEL CORN

2 c. brown sugar
1 c. butter
1/2 c. light corn syrup
1 tsp. salt
1 tsp. baking soda
1 tsp. butter flavoring
6 qt. popped corn

Boil brown sugar, butter, syrup and salt for 5 minutes. Remove from heat and add soda and butter flavoring. Pour over popped corn. Mix well and put into 2 large ungreased cookie sheets. Bake at 200 degrees for 1 hour, stirring every 15 minutes. Turn onto brown paper bag and store in airtight container.

STATE FAIR CORN DOGS

1 c. flour
3/4 c. yellow cornmeal
2 tbsp. sugar
2 tbsp. baking powder
1 tbsp. dry mustard
1 tsp. salt
1 c. milk
1 egg
2 tbsp. shortening

Mix dry ingredients. Cut in shortening. Add milk and slightly beaten egg. Mix quickly until nearly smooth. Pour batter into a tall glass for dunking hot dogs. Fry in hot deep fat until golden brown. 4 unhusked ears of corn

Discard any soiled outer pieces of husk. Soak corn in cold water 5 to 10 minutes to clean and moisten. Drain well, do not dry. Set unhusked corn directly on ceramic tray or in microproof serving dish. Cook on high for 11 to 12 minutes.

Let stand 3 minutes. Peel back husks, discard silk, recover with husks. Serve corn hot with butter and salt. For increased servings allow 3 to 4 minutes cooking time for each ear of corn. Cooking time: 11 to 12 minutes. butter Salt to taste

Discard any soiled outer pieces of husk. Soak corn in cold water 5 to 10 minutes to clean and moisten. Drain. Set unhusked corn directly on microproof serving dish. Cook (microwave) on high, 11 to 12 minutes. Let stand 3 minutes. Husk and serve hot with butter. Makes 4 servings.

STATE FAIR FAMOUS CHESS BROWNIES

2 sticks butter
4 eggs
3/4 c. sugar
1 1/2 tsp. vanilla
2 c. self-rising flour
1 c. nuts

Melt butter, pour in bowl with sugar and beat. Put 1 egg, beat after each. Add remaining ingredients, beat well. Bake at 350 degrees for 40 minutes. Bake in loaf pan.

STATE FAIR FRESH LEMONADE

4 lemons
1 c. sugar
Ice (as desired) Water

Cut lemons in half and squeeze juice from lemons. Pour into pitcher (Tupperware pitchers work best). Add sugar and ice. Shake to mix. Add water to make 1/2 gallon. Use of an inexpensive juicer makes the recipe go faster.

STATE FAIR HOT DOG (MICROWAVE)

1 jumbo hot dog
1 hot dog bun, split
Mustard
2 tbsp. sauerkraut, drained
Relish, chili, grated cheese or chopped onion

Slash both sides of hot dog in several places with a knife. Place on microproof plate and cook on High 1 minute or until hot. Place hot dog in bun. Add mustard, sauerkraut and selected garnish. Cook on High 15 seconds. Yield: 1.

STATE FAIR OF TEXAS POPPY SEED POUND CAKE

1 tbsp. poppy seed
1/4 c. milk
6 eggs
3 c. sugar
1 c. butter
1 c. buttermilk
1/4 tsp. soda
3 c. flour
2 tsp. vanilla extract
 GLAZE:
1 1/2 c. powdered sugar
1 tsp. melted butter
1 tsp. vanilla
1/2 c. milk

Soak poppy seeds in 1/4 cup milk. Separate eggs. Combine egg yolks, sugar, butter and cream well. Add poppy seeds and milk to buttermilk. Combine soda and flour. Add dry mixture to creamed mixture alternately with buttermilk. Beat egg whites until stiff. Fold into batter and add vanilla.

Pour into a greased bundt pan and bake at 325 degrees for 1 hour to 1 hour and 10 minutes. Remove from pan and drizzle glaze over the warm cake. Serves: 2 to 12!

STATE FAIR PEAR PIE

1/2 c. brown sugar, packed
2 tbsp. flour
1/2 tsp. cinnamon
Pinch of allspice
Pinch of cardamom
Pinch of nutmeg
Pinch of salt
6 c. peeled, sliced pears
2 tsp. lemon juice
1 1/2 tsp. vanilla extract Pie crust for 8 or 9 inch pie

In bowl, combine brown sugar, flour, spices and salt. Add pear slices, lemon juice and vanilla. Toss gently until well mixed. Pour fruit into pastry lined pie plate, mounding in center. Dot with butter. Brush rim of bottom crust with water. Cover with top crust. Fold edge under bottom crust. Flute edge. Cut small steam vents, brush with milk and sprinkle with sugar. Bake at 400 degrees for 15 minutes, then at 375 degrees for 45 to 50 minutes more.

STATE FAIR SLUSH

8 c. water
2 c. sugar (can be reduced)
1 (46 oz.) can pineapple juice
1 (6 oz.0 can frozen lemonade
1 (6 oz.) can frozen orange juice
4 ripe bananas
1 lg. 7-UP

Boil water and sugar; cool. Combine all of the above and freeze. (Can be frozen in milk cartons.) Makes about 1 gallon. Remove from freezer several hours ahead of serving to partially thaw. When serving, put half glass of slush in glass; fill with 7-UP. Recipe can be halved.

STATE FAIR SUGAR COOKIES

1 c. butter
1 c. vegetable oil
1 c. powdered sugar
1 c. granulated sugar
2 eggs
1 tsp. vanilla
4 c. flour
1 tsp. cream of tartar
1 tsp. baking soda
1 tsp. salt
Sugar (white granulated or colored for holidays)

Cream first 4 ingredients, then add eggs and vanilla. Sift together the remaining ingredients and add to dough. Chill dough. Roll 1 tablespoon dough in sugar. Place on ungreased cookie sheet. Press down on balls with glass dipped in sugar. Decorate with sprinkle if desired. Bake at 350 degrees for 12 minutes or until golden brown.

TRADITIONAL ENGLISH CHRISTMAS FAIRE!

CHRISTMAS PUDDING

1/2 lb. dark molasses sugar
14 oz. fresh white bread crumbs
1/2 lb. shredded beef suet
1 tsp. mixed spice
3/4 lb. sultanas
3/4 lb. raisins
1/2 tsp. salt
1/2 lb. currants
4 oz. candid peel, chopped
2 oz. blanched almonds finely chopped (optional)
2 lg. cooking apples, peeled, cored, and finely chopped Finely grated rind and juice of 1/2 lemon
2 eggs beaten
1/2 pint guinness or milk stout
Approximately 1/4 pt. milk
2 silver threepenny or, Sixpenny pieces, wrapped in foil!

Put the dry ingredients, dried fruit, candied peel and chopped almonds, if used, in a large mixing bowl and stir well to mix. Add the apples with the lemon rind and juice, eggs and Guinness or milk stout. Stir well to mix. Stir in enough milk to make a soft dropping consistency.

Pour the mixture into two greased 1 1/2 pint pudding basins. Bury one silver coin in each pudding. Cover the tops of the puddings with circles of greaseproof (waxed) paper, then with foil. Foil a pleat in the center and tie string around the rim. Leave overnight.

Place the basin in the top of a steamer or double boiler, or in a large pan of gently bubbling water and steam for 4 to 5 hours, topping up the water level from time to time during cooking.

Remove the basins carefully from the pan and leave until quite cold. Discard the foil and greaseproof paper and replace with fresh greaseproof paper and foil before storing. Stream again for about 2 hours before serving, with Brandy Butter.

WEST VIRGINIA STATE FAIR WINNING EGG CUSTARD PIE

6 eggs, beaten
1/2 stick melted butter
1 c. sugar
1 tbsp. self-rising flour
3 tbsp. plain flour
2 1/2 c. milk
1 1/2 tsp. vanilla

Mix all the above ingredients together. Pour into a deep dish pie crust. Bake at 350 degrees for 45-50 minutes.

WORLD'S FAIR CHICKEN

3 frying chickens, cut up
Salt and pepper
1 1/2 c. concentrated orange juice
1/2 c. chutney
1/2 tsp. cinnamon
Dash thyme
1/2 tsp. curry powder
1/2 c. almonds, slivered
1/2 c. white raisins

Season chicken with salt and pepper. Bake at 400 degrees for 45 minutes. Drain liquid. Combine orange juice, curry, chutney, cinnamon, and thyme. Cook 10 minutes. Pour sauce over chicken. Add almonds and raisins. Marinate 24 hours. To serve, heat thoroughly in a slow oven. Garnish platter with bananas, pineapple and mandarin oranges.

VANILLA BOURBON BREAD

2 cups all-purpose flour
1½ cups sugar
2 teaspoons baking powder
¾ teaspoon salt
1½ cups heavy cream
3 large eggs
2 tablespoons bourbon
1 tablespoon vanilla

Heat oven to 350 degrees. Grease a 9- by 5-inch loaf pan. Combine flour, sugar, baking powder and salt; set aside. Blend the cream, eggs, bourbon and vanilla until thoroughly mixed. Add to dry ingredients and stir by hand just until dry ingredients are evenly moistened. Pour into prepared pan. Bake at 350 degrees for 35 to 40 minutes or until a toothpick inserted in the center comes out clean. Cool in pan 10 minutes before removing to wire rack to cool completely.

TEX-MEX WON TON APPETIZERS

(Minnesota State Fair)
1 package small (3½- inch) won ton wraps
1 (12-ounce) package bulk sausage (any flavor)
1 (8-ounce) bottle of ranch dressing
3 tablespoons Tabasco Green Pepper Sauce
1 (8-ounce) shredded cheddar cheese
1 small jar pimientos
1 small can black olives, sliced
½ cup mild salsa

In a large skillet, brown the sausage until no longer pink; drain well and crumble. Place meat in a large mixing bowl. Heat oven to 350 degrees. Place won ton wraps in mini-muffin tins, shaping to form small cups. Bake 5 minutes. Remove from oven and set aside. Don't turn oven off.

Add ranch dressing and Tabasco sauce to crumbled meat. Stir in shredded cheese, pimientos, olives and salsa. Spoon mixture evenly into each won ton cup. Bake at 350 degrees for an additional 8 to 10 minutes. Serve hot. Make about 20 appetizers

PINEAPPLE CASHEW CHICKEN

(Michigan State Fair)
2 cubes low-sodium chicken bouillon
1 pound boneless, skinless chicken breast, cut into strips
¼ cup strawberry vinegar
1 (20-ounce) can pineapple tidbits, drained; juice reserved
1 medium green or red pepper
½ cup sliced onions
½ cup sliced carrots
1 cup broccoli florets
¾ cup cashews
Hot cooked rice

In a large nonstick skillet, brown chicken strips; add onion and cook 1 minute longer. Remove pan from heat.

Dissolve the chicken bouillon in the reserved pineapple juice; add the vinegar and stir well. Add to the browned chicken. Return pan to medium heat. Stir in broccoli, carrots, pepper and cashews. Cook until vegetables are crisp-tender. Add the pineapple tidbits and serve over hot rice.

APPLE-CRANBERRY COFFEE CAKE

(San Diego County Fair)

Cake:

3 cups all-purpose flour
¾ teaspoon baking soda
1 tablespoon baking powder
½ teaspoon salt
¾ cup butter, softened
1 cup sugar
½ cup firmly packed brown sugar
1 teaspoon vanilla
3 large eggs
1½ cups sour cream

Filling:

1 cup dried cranberries
2 medium apples, peeled, cored and shredded
1/3 cup sugar
¾ teaspoon cinnamon
½ cup chopped, toasted walnuts
2 tablespoons cold butter

Heat oven to 350 degrees. Grease and flour a 10-inch Bundt pan. In a large bowl, combine flour, soda, baking powder and salt. In a large mixing bowl, cream butter, sugar and brown sugar until light and fluffy. Blend in vanilla. Add eggs, one at a time, beating well after each addition. Add flour mixture to creamed mixture, alternating with sour cream. Mix to blend after each addition. In small bowl mix all filling ingredients, except the butter; set aside.

Spoon one-third of the cake batter into the Bundt pan. Spoon half of the cranberry-apple filling over batter and dot with 1 tablespoon of butter. Spoon second third of cake batter over filling. Spoon remaining filling over batter and dot with remaining tablespoon of butter. Spoon in remaining cake batter.

Bake at 350 degrees for 55 to 70 minutes or until cake tests done when a long toothpick or skewer is inserted in the center. Remove from oven and cool in pan 10 minutes. Invert onto a cooling rack. Cool completely, then top with glaze.

Glaze

2 cups powdered sugar
1 tablespoon, plus 1 teaspoon fresh lemon juice
1 tablespoon milk
2 tablespoon butter, melted
½ teaspoon vanilla

Mix all until smooth. Drizzle over top of cake. Garnish with dried cranberries and toasted walnuts, if desired.

BREAKFAST ENCHILADAS

(Iowa State Fair)
2 cups turkey ham, finely diced
½ cup chopped green onions
10 (8-inch) flour tortillas
2 cups (8 ounces) shredded cheddar cheese
1 tablespoon all-purpose flour
2 cups half-and-half
6 eggs, beaten
¼ teaspoon salt

Combine ham and onions. Place about 1/3 cup of the mixture down the center of each tortilla. Top with 2 tablespoons of cheese. Roll up and place seam side down in a greased 9- by 13-inch glass baking dish.

In a medium-size mixing bowl, combine flour, half-and-half, eggs and salt, mixing until smooth. Pour mixture over filled tortillas. Cover with plastic wrap and refrigerate overnight.

To prepare: Remove pan from fridge and let stand for 30 minutes. Heat oven to 350 degrees. Cover pan with foil. Bake at 350 degrees for 25 minutes. Uncover and bake an additional 10 minutes. Sprinkle with

remaining cheese and bake 3 minutes longer or until cheese is melted. Let stand 10 minutes

Oriental Summertime Salad

2 packages ramen noodles (discard seasoning packet and break noodles into bite-size pieces)
1/2 cup (1 stick) margarine
1/4 cup sesame seeds
1/2 cup vinegar
3/4 cup sugar
1 cup vegetable oil
2 tablespoons Kikkoman's naturally brewed soy sauce
3 pounds napa cabbage, thinly sliced
6 green onions, sliced
1 cup sliced strawberries
1/2 cup blueberries
1/2 cup pineapple tidbits
1/2 cup mandarin oranges
1/2 cup sliced honey roasted almonds

In large skillet over medium heat, saute broken noodles in margarine, stirring until brown, 3 to 4 minutes. Add sesame seeds and brown 1 minute. Set aside.

In small bowl, whisk together vinegar, sugar and oil until sugar is dissolved. Add soy sauce and set aside.

Shortly before serving, combine noodles with remaining ingredients except soy sauce mixture. Mix just until combined. Just prior to serving, pour soy sauce mixture over salad and mix. Makes 6 servings.

Barbecue Sauce

2 tablespoons vegetable oil
1/2 cup chopped onion
2 tablespoons minced garlic
1 teaspoon ground cumin
1/4 teaspoon cayenne pepper
1 cup ketchup
1/2 cup malt vinegar
1/4 cup soy sauce
1/4 cup packed dark brown sugar
2 tablespoons Worcestershire sauce
1/4 teaspoon liquid smoke, preferably natural

In medium saucepan, heat oil. Add onion, garlic, cumin and cayenne pepper and cook over medium heat 5 minutes.

Stir in remaining ingredients and simmer, stirring occasionally, until slightly thickened, about 10 minutes. Makes 2 cups.

Old-Fashioned Sausage and Peppers

1/4 cup extra-virgin olive oil
2 cloves garlic, thinly sliced
1 large red onion, cut into 2-inch chunks
2 red bell peppers, cored, seeded and cut in 2-inch chunks
2 green bell peppers, cored, seeded and cut in 2-inch chunks
4 hot Italian sausages
4 sweet Italian sausages
1 cup crushed canned Italian plum tomatoes
1 1/2 cups Chianti
Pinch of dried oregano
Salt and black pepper to taste

Divide oil between 2 large skillets with lids; heat over medium heat. Divide garlic, onion and peppers between skillets and cook, stirring as needed, until onion is translucent, about 5 minutes. Add sausages, 4 to a skillet, and cook about 4 minutes more until sausages begin to brown. Add tomatoes, wine, oregano and a pinch of salt to pans. Cover, bring to simmer for about 25 minutes, until peppers are soft. Season with salt and pepper. Serve with crusty bread. Makes about 6 servings.

Beef and Rice Enchiladas

1 pound ground round
1 medium onion, chopped
1/2 cup chopped green bell pepper
1 tablespoon minced garlic
1 can (6 ounces) tomato paste
3/4 cup water
1 cup cooked white rice
3 cups shredded cheddar cheese (divided)
1 1/2 teaspoons dried oregano
1/2 teaspoon dried thyme
1/2 teaspoon fennel seed
1 teaspoon garlic salt
1 tablespoon chili powder
12 flour tortillas (about 10-inches) warmed
8 ounces picante sauce or salsa
1 can (about 10 ounces) enchilada sauce

In large saute pan, cook ground round, onion, bell pepper and garlic until meat is thoroughly cooked. Remove from heat and drain excess liquid. Add tomato paste, water, rice, 2 cups cheese, picante sauce and seasonings. Cook over low heat until mixture is thickened, about 10 minutes.

Spread 1/2 cup of beef mixture on each tortilla and roll it up.

Pour 1/4 cup sauce on bottom of 9-inch baking pan. Place enchiladas, seam side down, in pan. Pour rest of sauce over burritos and sprinkle with remaining 1 cup cheese. Bake in 350-degree oven 8 to 10 minutes or until heated through and cheese melts. Makes 4 servings.

Pina Colada Bread

2 cups flour
2 teaspoons baking powder
1 teaspoon baking soda
1/4 teaspoon salt
1/2 cup (1 stick) butter, room temperature
1 cup sugar
2 eggs
1/2 teaspoon dried minced lemon peel
3/4 cup sweetened flaked coconut
1 cup crushed pineapple (spooned out of the can, with some juice)
2 tablespoons Kahlua
1/4 cup milk

Glaze (see recipe)

In bowl, combine flour, baking powder, baking soda and salt. Set aside.

In another bowl, cream butter and sugar. Add eggs, one at a time, mixing well after each addition. Add lemon peel, coconut, pineapple, Kahlua and milk. Mix well.

Slowly add dry ingredients to butter mixture. Add in 1/2 cup portions, mixing well after each addition.

Preheat oven to 350 degrees. Grease bottoms of 4 tea-sized (6-by-3-inch) loaf pans. Divide batter among pans and bake 25 minutes or until done.

While breads bake, prepare glaze.

When loaves are done, remove from oven and place on cooling rack. Pour glaze over breads while still warm. Let breads cool in pans. Cool then remove from pans. Make 4 breads.

Glaze

1/2 cup sugar
1/4 cup pineapple juice
1/2 teaspoon Kahlua

Combine sugar, juice and Kahlua in saucepan. Cook over low heat until sugar dissolves, 4 to 5 minutes. Remove from heat and set aside until breads are done.

Marbled Maple Cheesecake

Crust (see recipe)

2 pounds (four 8-ounce packages) cream cheese, room temperature
1/2 cup plus 2 tablespoons pure maple syrup (divided)
1/4 cup plus 3 tablespoons chopped pecans (divided)
3 eggs, lightly beaten
1/4 teaspoon vanilla extract
4 ounces semi-sweet chocolate, melted

Make crust. Let cool while preparing filling.

Preheat oven to 275 degrees.

Beat cream cheese until smooth. Beat in 1/2 cup maple syrup, 1/4 cup of the pecans, eggs and vanilla. Pour into prepared crust. Drizzle melted chocolate over top and swirl with knife.

Bake 1 hour and 30 minutes or until set. Let cool.

Spread remaining 2 tablespoons maple syrup over top and sprinkle with remaining 3 tablespoons chopped pecans. Chill at least 6 hours. Makes 24 servings.

Crust

1/2 cup (1 stick) butter, cut into pieces
2/3 cup firmly packed brown sugar
3/4 teaspoon vanilla extract
1 egg
1 1/2 cups flour
1 cup chopped pecans

Preheat oven to 325 degrees.

In food processor, blend butter, brown sugar and vanilla until well mixed. Add egg and flour and blend until dough just forms. Transfer to bowl and gently knead in pecans. Press into 9-inch springform pan and bake 30 minutes. When done, remove from oven and let cool.

Frango Chocolate Cappuccino Mousse Pie

1 cup flour
1/2 cup powdered sugar
1/2 cup (1 stick) butter, room temperature
1/2 cup finely chopped pecans
1 package (3 ounces) cream cheese, room temperature
4 teaspoons instant Amaretto-flavored cappuccino powder
1 teaspoon vanilla extract
1 1/2 cups melted, then cooled Frango chocolates (about 33 mints)
2 cups whipped cream
Frango chocolates and/or pecan halves for garnish

Preheat oven to 350 degrees.

Combine flour, powdered sugar, butter and pecans. Mix using 2 knives. Pat onto bottom of and up sides of 9-inch pie plate. Bake 15 minutes or until done. Remove from oven and cool.

Combine cream cheese, cappuccino powder, vanilla and melted chocolate. Mix well. Fold in whipped cream. Spoon into cooled crust and refrigerate at least 3 hours before serving. Garnish with chocolates and/or pecans. Makes 6 servings.

Frango Raspberry Mint Brownies

12 Frango mint chocolate candies (divided)
1/3 cup corn oil
1 cup sugar
2 eggs
1 teaspoon raspberry extract (optional)
3/4 cup sifted flour
1/2 teaspoon baking powder
1/2 teaspoon salt
1/2 cup coarsely chopped nuts (optional) Frosting layer (see recipe)
1 tablespoon butter

Preheat oven to 350 degrees. Grease 8-inch square baking pan.

In saucepan, melt 6 chocolate candies in oil over low heat, just until chocolate melts. Remove from heat and beat in sugar, eggs and extract. Set aside.

In sifter, combine flour, baking powder and salt and sift directly into pan with chocolate mixture. Add nuts if desired. Spread mixture into prepared pan. Bake 25 to 30 minutes or until done. When done, remove from oven and cool.

While brownies bake, make frosting layer.

When brownies are cooled, frost and refrigerate 30 minutes or until set. Once chilled, remove from refrigerator.

In microwave-safe bowl combine remaining 6 Frango chocolates and butter. Microwave until melted, then pour over frosting layer. Spread to cover. Refrigerate until chocolate layer is set. Cut into squares when cool. Makes 12 servings.

Frosting layer

1/2 cup (1 stick) butter, room temperature
4 cups powdered sugar
1/4 cup milk (about)
1 teaspoon vanilla extract
3 tablespoons raspberry jam (preferably seedless) A few drops red food coloring

In bowl, beat butter and powdered sugar, adding milk as needed to make a fluffy frosting, about 5 minutes. Beat in vanilla, jam and food coloring, if using.

MEXICALI SNACK MIX

1-1/2 c. roasted salted peanuts
1-1/2 c. bite-size wheat or corn square cereal (chex)
1 c. sunflower seeds
1 c. cornnuts or pretzel nuggets
1/4 c. butter or margarine, melted
2 tsps. chili powder
1/4 tsp. ground cumin
1/4 tsp. red pepper
1/8 tsp. garlic powder

Combine 1st 4 ingredients in jelly roll pan and stir. Drizzle butter over top and stir. Sprinkle with seasonings and stir well. Bake 350° for 20 minutes. Stir after 10 minutes.

Makes approximately 5 cups

SPICY PEANUT DIP

3 garlic cloves, peeled
3/4" (inch) piece fresh ginger, peeled
2 c. unsalted dry roasted peanuts
1/4 – 1/2 tsp. Oriental chili paste
2 tsps. sugar, or more to taste
2-1/2 T. Chinese rice wine vinegar
3 tbsps. soy sauce
1/4 c. Oriental sesame oil
1/4 c. water
1 T. sliced green onion, green part – for garnish

In a food processor with the motor running and the metal blade in place, drop garlic and ginger through the feed tube and process until chopped fine, about 20 seconds. Remove and reserve.

Process 1-1/3 cups of peanuts until smooth, about 3 minutes. Add remaining peanuts, gingergarlic mixture, and remaining ingredients except green onion. Process until combined, about 15 seconds.

Transfer mixture to a serving dish and garnish with green onion. Serve with crackers or vegetables.

Serves 6

CHIPOTLE DIP (pronounced, chih poht lay, sometimes spelled chipolte)

Chipotle chiles are actually dried, smoked jalapenos, medium thick flesh, smoky, earthy and sweet in flavor with a hint of tobacco and chocolate. They can be bought packed in adobo, (chile stewed in lightly seasoned sauce made from ground chiles, herbs, tomatoes and vinegar).

2 green onions, finely chopped
1 c. mayonnaise
1/2 c. sour cream
1 tsp. fresh lemon juice
2-3 canned chipotle chiles in adobo
1/4 tsp. adobo sauce from can

In a bowl whisk together onions, mayonnaise, sour cream and lemon juice and set aside.

Wearing gloves, finely chop chipotles and add to bowl along with sauce. Season to taste with salt, if desired. Serve with bell pepper strips, crackers or chips.

Makes about 1-1/2 cups. Will keep, covered and refrigerated, up to 3 days.

FRUIT SMOOTHIE

2 c. plain yogurt
2 c. milk
2 c. frozen or pulp of ripe pineapple, mangoes, strawberries or peaches
juice of 1 lemon
1-2 tsps. sugar

Place all in a blender and process until smooth. Serve over ice. Serves 4

SANTA FE PASTA SALAD

16 oz. pkg. Rotini pasta, cooked, drained, tossed with a little oil and chilled

Dressing

1-1/4 c. V-8 juice
1-1/2 tbsps. olive oil
1 tbsp. red wine vinegar
1-1/2 tsps. chili powder
3/4 tsp. paprika
1/2 tsp. salt
1/4 tsp. black pepper
1/2 c. grated Parmesan cheese
1/2 c. cooked yellow corn kernels
1/3 c. chopped cilantro
1/4 c. chopped green onion
2 tbsps. diced red bell pepper
2 tbsps. diced green bell pepper
1 chicken breast fillet, cooked and diced, optional

Whisk all of the dressing ingredients together in a small bowl. Cover and chill the dressing until needed.

Pour pasta into a large bowl. Add the dressing, then toss. Add the remaining ingredients to the pasta, and toss until combined. Cover and chill for several hours before serving.

PASTA PRIMAVERA

1 lb. cooked spaghetti or spaghettini
1/2 c. vegetable or olive oil
2 garlic cloves, chopped
1 onion, chopped
1 large sweet red pepper, diced
1 large sweet green pepper, diced
1 medium zucchini, thinly sliced
1/4 c. caper, rinsed and chopped
3 ozs. grated Parmesan cheese
salt and pepper to taste

Heat oil over medium heat in a 10" saute pan or 12" skillet. Add garlic and onion and cook 1 minute. Add peppers and cook 1-2 minutes or until crisp-tender. Season with salt and pepper. Add zucchini and pasta and capers to skillet and heat thoroughly. Transfer to large serving platter, sprinkle with 2 tbsps. Parmesan cheese and serve hot with remaining Parmesan on the side. Serves 3-4

PASTA WITH TUNA SAUCE

14 oz. can tuna in oil
3 tbsps. olive oil
2-3 cloves garlic, minced
15 oz. can tomato paste
1-1/2 to 2 cans water (use tomato paste can)
2 tbsps. parsley
salt and pepper or red pepper flakes to taste
1 lb. spaghetti or any shaped pasta
grated Parmesan cheese

In a saucepan, add oil from tuna and olive oil and heat over low heat. Add garlic and saute just until golden, do not brown. Stir in tomato paste and cook for 5 minutes, stirring. Add water, stir, bring to a slow simmer, cover and cook for 20 minutes, stirring often. Add tuna and break up in the sauce. Heat for 5-10 minutes. Add half of parsley, season to taste. Cook pasta according to package directions, drain and place in serving bowl. Pour sauce over top, toss, sprinkle with remaining parsley, and cheese.

BLAZING BROWNIES

1 box brownie mix

crushed hot pepper or ground cayenne pepper to taste

Follow directions on box. Mix pepper in at the end, just before batter goes into pan. Bake according to directions.

NOTE: Suggest starting with ½ teaspoon of pepper. With each box of brownie mix, try adding more pepper to suit your taste.

CARAMEL SAUCE

½ cup butter or margarine
½ cup firmly packed brown sugar
½ cup granulated sugar
½ cup evaporated milk
1 tbsp. Vanilla extract

Combine butter, sugars and milk in a medium saucepan.

Stirring constantly, cook over low heat until butter melts and sugars dissolve.

Increase heat to medium and bring to a boil.

Stirring constantly, boil about 9 minutes or until thickened.

Remove from heat and stir in vanilla. Serve warm.

Makes about 1-1/2 cups.

(This keeps well in refrigerator. Heat before serving over dessert.)

2 cups all-purpose flour
1 1/2 tablespoons white sugar
1/2 teaspoon salt
1/2 cup butter
1 (.25 ounce) package active dry yeast
1/4 cup warm water
1/2 cup milk, scalded and cooled
1 egg yolk
2 tablespoons butter, softened
2 cups white sugar
4 tablespoons melted butter
3 1/2 teaspoons ground cinnamon
1/4 cup chopped walnuts

Mix flour, sugar and salt. Cut in butter, as for pastry.

Soften yeast in water. Combine milk, egg yolk and softened yeast. Add to flour mixture and mix well.

Cover dough and refrigerate for at least 2 hours.

Place dough on a lightly floured cutting board and knead lightly. Cover with a cloth and allow to rest for 10 minutes.

Roll dough into a rectangle, 10x18 inches, and brush with soft butter. Mix 1/2 cup sugar and 2 teaspoons cinnamon and sprinkle evenly over dough. Roll as for jelly roll, sealing the edge. The roll should be 18 inches long.

Cut dough into 1-inch slices.

Mix remaining sugar and cinnamon on a large square of waxed paper or aluminum foil. Place slices, one at a time, on sugar mixture and roll into 5-inch balls.

Sprinkle nuts on top and press gently.

Place dough on ungreased cookie sheets, brush with melted butter and sprinkle with about 1 teaspoon of the sugar-cinnamon mixture.

2 cups all-purpose flour
1 1/2 tablespoons white sugar
1/2 teaspoon salt
1/2 cup butter
1 (.25 ounce) package active dry yeast 1/4 cup warm water
1/2 cup milk, scalded and cooled 1 egg yolk
2 tablespoons butter, softened
2 cups white sugar
4 tablespoons melted butter
3 1/2 teaspoons ground cinnamon 1/4 cup chopped walnuts

Mix flour, sugar and salt. Cut in butter, as for pastry.

Soften yeast in water. Combine milk, egg yolk and softened yeast. Add to flour mixture and mix well.

Cover dough and refrigerate for at least 2 hours.

Place dough on a lightly floured cutting board and knead lightly. Cover with a cloth and allow to rest for 10 minutes.

Roll dough into a rectangle, 10x18 inches, and brush with soft butter. Mix 1/2 cup sugar and 2 teaspoons cinnamon and sprinkle evenly over dough. Roll as for jelly roll, sealing the edge. The roll should be 18 inches long.

Cut dough into 1-inch slices.

Mix remaining sugar and cinnamon on a large square of waxed paper or aluminum foil. Place slices, one at a time, on sugar mixture and roll into 5-inch balls.

Sprinkle nuts on top and press gently.

Place dough on ungreased cookie sheets, brush with melted butter and sprinkle with about 1 teaspoon of the sugar-cinnamon mixture.

A Plus Fair Corn Dogs

1 quart oil for deep frying
1 cup all-purpose flour
2/3 cup yellow cornmeal
1/4 cup white sugar
1 1/2 teaspoons baking powder
1 teaspoon salt
2 tablespoons bacon drippings
1 egg, beaten
1 1/4 cups buttermilk
1/2 teaspoon baking soda
2 pounds hot dogs
wooden sticks

Heat oil in a deep fryer to 365 degrees F (185 degrees C).

In a large bowl, stir together the flour, cornmeal, sugar, baking powder and salt. Make a well in the center, and pour in the egg, buttermilk, and baking soda. Mix until everything is smooth and well blended.

Pat the hot dogs dry with paper towels so that the batter will stick. Insert wooden sticks into the ends. Dip the hot dogs in the batter one at a time, shaking off the excess. Deep fry a few at a time in the hot oil until they are as brown as you like them. Drain on paper towels or serve on paper plates.

State Fair Pasta

A hearty dish reminiscent of the sausage & peppers served at the fair - served on top of pasta instead of a bun!

8 ounces fettuccine (or your favorite pasta)
salt
3-4 tablespoons butter
2 large Italian sausages (about 1/2 lb)
1/4 large green bell pepper, sliced
1/4 large red bell pepper, sliced
1/2 small white onion, sliced
3 cloves garlic, minced
1 teaspoon cajun seasoning

In a large, preferably cast-iron skillet, brown sausage links on all sides (this makes them easier to slice).

Remove, slice, and return to pan.

Cook sliced sausage over medium-high heat until cooked through; remove and set aside. Melt 1 tbsp butter and saute garlic for 2-3 minutes.

Add onion, peppers, and cajun seasoning.

Stir frequently, adding more butter as needed to keep the mixture from drying out. Meanwhile, cook pasta in boiling salted water until al dente.

When the onions and peppers have softened, add in the cooked sausage and heat through. Drain pasta, top each serving with a big spoonful of the sausage, onions,& peppers, and serve.

State Fair Potato Salad

Drizzling sweet pickle juice over the warm potatoes is the secret to this delicious potato salad. Tastes like a contrest entree at the State Fair! From Bon Appetit.

3 1/2 lbs red potatoes, peeled,cut into 3/4 inch pieces
1/4 cup juice, from jar of sweet pickles
3/4 cup mayonnaise
1/3 cup buttermilk
4 teaspoons Dijon mustard
1 teaspoon sugar
1/2 teaspoon ground black pepper
3 hard-boiled eggs, peeled,chopped
1/2 cup chopped red onions
1/2 cup chopped celery
1/2 cup chopped sweet gherkins

cook potatoes in large pot of boiling salted water until just tender, about 10 minutes. drain; transfer to large bowl.

Drizzle pickle juice over potatoes and toss gently.

Cool to room temperature.

Whisk mayonnaise, buttermilk, mustard, sugar and pepper in medium bowl to blend. Pour over potatoes.

Add eggs, onion, celery, and pickles and toss gently to blend.

Season to taste with salt.

Can be made 8 hours ahead.

Chill.

Strawberry Rhubarb Pie

The title says it all...we make this every time our rhubarb is ready to be picked...many times each summer and it's gone before it's even cooled!

4 cups rhubarb, cut into 1 inch pieces
2 cups strawberries, washed and cut up
5 tablespoons dry tapioca
3 cups sugar
1 teaspoon nutmeg
1/2 teaspoon salt
1 teaspoon cinnamon
1/2 teaspoon ground cloves
1 teaspoon lemon juice
5 teaspoons butter
1 pie crust (I use Pillsbury ready-made)

Combine rhubarb, strawberries, sugar, and tapioca in large bowl.

Let mixture sit for 20 minutes at room temperature to dissolve sugar and tapioca. Stir every few minutes.

Meanwhile, preheat oven to 450 and put pie crust in pie tin.

After sitting time, add nutmeg, salt, cinnamon, cloves, and lemon juice to mixture. Stir well and put into crust, draining excess liquid.

Dot top of mixture with pats of butter then place crust on top and seal edges.

Place a cookie sheet under pie to catch drips.

Bake at 450 for 30 minutes, then 425 for another 30 minutes, then 350 for 15 minutes or until done.

You might have to cover edges of crust with foil or a pie guard to prevent crust from burning- Will thicken as it cools.

New York State Apple pie

1 pie crust (For crust use whatever you are comfortable with-I am happy with those you can find in the dairy case)
5 cups apples, peeled and sliced (your choice)
1 teaspoon fresh lemon juice
3/4 cup sugar
1/4 teaspoon salt
2 tablespoons flour
1 teaspoon ground cinnamon
2 tablespoons margarine

Sprinkle lemon juice over apple slices.

Combine sugar, salt, flour,cinnamon and nutmeg in a mixing bowl. Sprinkle over apple slices.

Toss apples and flour mixture until apple slices are fully coated. Arrange into bottom prepared crust.

dot with margarine.

Cover with top crust and fold under and crimp.

cut slits into top crustand dust with sugar if desired.

Bake at 375 degrees for 50 minutes

Silver State Brownies

1 cup margarine
2 cups sugar
4 eggs
2 teaspoons vanilla
1/2 cup cocoa
1 1/2 cups flour
1/2 cup chopped nuts mini chocolate chips

20-24 servings 1 9x13 pan Change size or US/metric Change to: 9x13 pan US Metric

Cream margarine, add sugar.

Beat eggs and add to mixture, add vanilla.

Mix cocoa and flour together and stir into mixture.

Stir in nuts.

Pour into 9 x 13 greased and floured pan; sprinkle with mini chocolate chips. Bake at 350 degrees for 25 to 30 minutes.

Sunshine State Carrots

1 lb baby carrots
1/2 cup orange juice
2 tablespoons butter
2 tablespoons honey
1 tablespoon cornstarch
1 tablespoon water
1/3 cup chopped walnuts

4 servings Change size or US/metric Change to: servings US Metric

Place carrots in saucepan with small amount of water, cook until just tender crisp, (I like to steam them).

Drain.

Stir in orange juice, butter, honey, and cornstarch mixed with the water.

heat stirring, until thickened, Sprinkle with walnuts, Serve.

Empire State Muffins

These muffins are really packed with lots of good stuff. I am not sure where I got this recipe (probably either the newspaper or my mother). They are very versitle can add or substitute alot of ingredients.

2 cups shredded unpeeled apples
1 1/3 cups sugar
1 cup chopped cranberries or any dried fruit or raisins or blueberries
1 cup shredded carrots
1 cup chopped nuts
2 1/2 cups all-purpose flour
1 tablespoon baking powder
2 teaspoons baking soda
1/2 teaspoon salt
2 teaspoons cinnamon
2 eggs, lightly beaten
1/2 cup vegetable oil

18 Muffins Change size or US/metric Change to: Muffins US Metric

In a large bowl combine apples and sugar. Gently fold in cranberries, carrots and nuts. Combine dry ingredients and add to bowl. Mix well to moisten dry ingredients.

Combine eggs and oil and stir into apple mixture. Fill 18 greased muffin tins 2/3 full.

Bake at 375 for 20- 25 minutes.

Cool 5 minutes before removing from tins.

Virginia State Peanut Soup

This soup is a favorite in my neck of the woods. This is high in calories and it will fill you up quickly. It is the kind of soup that will stick to your ribs.

1 (9 1/4 ounce) jar dry roasted peanuts
2 cups water
2 cups milk
2 (5 1/2 g) packages instant chicken broth
1 tablespoon dried chives

Chop nuts into a fine mixture Use a food processor.

(If it turns into a puree or paste--this is fine) Add peanut mixture and the rest of ingredients into a medium saucepan.

Heat, stirring constantly, for 5 to 20 mins.

Serve in small bowls.

Vermont State Police Pears

6 pears
1 lemon
maple syrup
8 fluid ounces white grape juice

Choose a casserole or baking dish with just enough room to lay the pears head to tail in a single layer.

Peel the pears thinly, leaving the stalks on, and then immediately roll each one in a saucer containing the juice of the lemon.

Put the pears into the dish.

Spoon on a scant 4 tablespoons of maple syrup and add any lemon juice remaining in the saucer. Bring the grape juice to simmering point and pour it over the pears.

Cover the dish and bake at 350°F until the fruit is beautifully tender.

How long this will take varies enormously- 1 hour is enough for semi-ripe dessert pears; 3 hours or more may be needed for pears that are so hard that they seem to be carved from wood. Baste the pears frequently as they bake and turn them occasionally to encourage even cooking. When the pears are ready, transfer them to a serving dish, standing them upright. Boil the cooking liquid until it turns syrupy and is reduced by about half.

Stir in an extra tablespoon or two of maple if you think a little more sweetness is desirable but avoid the temptation to make the juices too sweet; the appeal of the dish lies in its fruitiness. Spoon the syrupy glaze over the pears.

Serve warm or cold.

Ohio State Buckeye Candy

1 lb confectioners' sugar
2/3 lb peanut butter (smooth variety)
6 tablespoons unsalted butter (softened)
1/2 lb semisweet chocolate
1/2 lb milk chocolate
1 tablespoon shredded paraffin wax

Blend sugar, peanut butter and butter together thoroughly.

Roll mixture into walnut-sized balls and insert a toothpick into each.

Place balls on a waxed paper lined cookie sheet and then put them in the freezer for about 10 minutes, or until firm.

Melt chocolate and paraffin in a double boiler.

Holding onto the toothpick, dip each chilled peanut butter ball into the melted chocolate, leaving a small round area near the toothpick. This will be the "eye" of the buckeye. The dipping of each ball should be done quickly so the warm chocolate does not thaw the peanut butter too much. This can cause the ball to slide off the toothpick and into the chocolate.

Place a fresh liner of waxed paper on the cookie sheet and put the buckeys on it. Refrigerate at least one-half hour before serving. You can then place the buckeyes in a container. For best results, keep them refrigerated until you serve them.

State Famous Deep Fried Walleye

1 cup finely crushed soda cracker crumbs
1/2 cup all-purpose flour
1/2 teaspoon garlic powder
1/2 teaspoon seasoning salt (use your favorite)
6 skinned walleyed pike fillet
2 large eggs
1 tablespoon water
vegetable shortening

Mix cracker crumbs flour garlic and seasoning salt in a medium bowl

Scramble the eggs and mix in the water in a small bowl

Melt shortening in deep frier and heat to 380 degrees

Put Walleye fillets in the egg mixture Put Walleye fillets in the crumb mixture and coat until you can't see the fish Put in deep frier and cook until golden brown and flaky Serve with lemon wedges and tartar sauce

Hyderabadi Khatti Dal (Mango Lentil Curry from the Indian state)

250 g yellow lentils, cleaned, washed and drained (Toovar dal)
2 raw mangoes, peeled, de-seeded and chopped
3 tomatoes, peeled and chopped
3-5 fresh curry leaves
100 g fresh coriander leaves
2 pinches turmeric powder
4 cloves garlic
2 teaspoons red chili powder
salt
3 tablespoons oil
2 teaspoons cumin seeds
1 teaspoon mustard seeds
5 green chilies

Put the first three ingredients in a pressure cooker.

Pressure cook for upto 2-3 whistles.

Remove from flame and let out the steam.

Mix the cooked lentils with water using a wooden spoon. Boil the mixture for 5 minutes.

Heat oil in a pan.

Add cumin seeds and mustard seeds.

Allow to splutter.

Once they stop spluttering, add curry leaves.

Stir-fry until fragrant.

Add garlic and stir-fry until the raw smell is gone.

Mix in the red chilli and turmeric powders and the corriander leaves. Fry till it turns slightly brown.

Pour over the boiled lentils.

Serve hot over cooked white rice.

Enjoy a hearty lunch!

County Fair Pie

1/2 cup butter or margarine, melted
1 cup sugar
1/2 cup all-purpose flour
2 eggs
1 teaspoon vanilla
1 cup coarsely chopped walnuts
1 cup semi-sweet chocolate chips (6 oz)
1/2 cup butterscotch chips
1 unbaked 9 inch pie shell

In a mixing bowl, beat the butter, sugar, flour, eggs and vanilla until well blended. Stir in nuts and chips.

Pour into pie shell.

Bake at 325 for 1 hour or until golden brown.

Cool.

Fair Funnel Cakes

3 eggs
1/4 cup sugar
2 cups whole milk
3 2/3 cups all-purpose flour
1/2 teaspoon salt
2 teaspoons baking powder

Beat together eggs and sugar. Add milk slowly and beat. Add all dry ingredients, beat until smooth. Pour batter in a funnel--hold the hole closed w/ your finger. Next, remove finger and creat designs while pouring it into the hot oil. BE VERY CAREFUL!!!!!!! (2 inches of oil). Turn onto other side until both sides are golden brown. Drain on paper towels and sprinkle w/ powdered sugar. We also like to add cinnamon as well.

Yummy!!

PS...I highly recommend you make a double batch!

Chicken Scarborough Fair

4 whole chicken breasts, halved lengthwise
2 cups buttermilk
1/4 cup butter
2 medium onions, sliced thin
4 cloves garlic, sliced thin
4 strips bacon, chopped small
1 teaspoon salt
1 teaspoon pepper
2 cups marsala wine or sherry wine
2 tablespoons flour
1 teaspoon Italian parsley (chopped)
1 teaspoon dried sage (powder or crushed leaves)
1 tablespoon dried rosemary (crushed)
1 (4 ounce) package Philadelphia Cream cheese

To prepare chicken: Use a whole breast (1/2 breast per person) with the back removed, split lengthwise at the breast bone.

Remove skin, salt and pepper each piece.

Place in a large bowl.

Add 2 cups buttermilk to tenderize for about an hour.

In a black iron skillet on the stovetop, over medium heat, melt 1/2 stick of butter. Add onions, garlic and bacon; cook just until onions are translucent about 7 minutes. Remove from pan and set aside.

Place buttermilk-coated pieces of chicken in hot skillet to quickly get some color. Remove and repeat with the remaining chicken.

Cook just until pieces have a nice golden brown color, approximately 5 minutes; remove and set aside.

Add wine (sherry) to deglaze the brown bits of chicken flavors from the pan, stirring to loosen. Let this cook for 5 minutes to burn off the alcohol.

Add onion mixture, parsley, sage, rosemary.

Stir in cream cheese.

Dissolve flour in 1/4 cup of water; add to the sauce.

Cook until just slightly thickened.

Adjust salt and pepper to taste.

Arrange the chicken pieces in a 16" roasting dish and pour the sauce over the chicken. Cover with aluminum foil and cook in a 350 degree oven for 20 minutes.

It makes an amazing sauce to serve over rice.

**You can substitute the wine or sherry with either apple or orange juice, add slivered almonds or mushrooms for diversity.

County Fair Banana Cream Pie

Nut Crust

2 cups pecans
1 cup butter, softened
3 cups flour
1 egg, beaten
1/2 cup sugar

Chocolate Filling

1 cup chocolate chips
1/2 cup unsalted butter
1 tablespoon light corn syrup
1 teaspoon vanilla

Banana Cream

1 cup milk
4 egg yolks
1 cup sugar
5 tablespoons flour
3 tablespoons unsalted butter
1 tablespoon rum or 1 teaspoon vanilla
2 bananas
1/2 lemon, juice of
2 cups heavy cream
pecans, Chopped (optional)

12 servings 2 pies Change size or US/metric Change to: pies US Metric

For the crust: Chop pecans very fine, preferably in a food processor fitted with a metal blade. Place in bowl with other crust ingredients and mix until well blended.

Divide in half and press into the bottom of 2 pie pans.

Chill 30 minutes.

Bake the pie crusts for 25 minutes at 350 degrees.

Cool completely.

For chocolate layer: Melt chocolate with butter and corn syrup in the top of a double boiler set over hot, not boiling water.

Stir frequently.

Remove from heat and cool, then stir in vanilla.

Divide between cooked pie crusts and spread evenly.

For Filling: Heat milk in a medium size saucepan over medium heat to scald. Beat the egg yolks and gradually add sugar.

Then beat in flour.

Gradually stir in hot milk.

Transfer to medium saucepan and cook, stirring constantly over medium high heat (use a whisk). The mixture will lump as it begins to thicken.

Bring the mixture to a boil and boil 1 minute, stirring constantly.

Remove from the pan from heat and continue to stir until the mixture is smooth. Then, beat in butter and optional rum.

Cool to room temperature.

Peel the bananas, slice very thin and toss with lemon juice.

Whip 1 cup of the cream until it is firm but not stiff.

Mix about 1/4 of the cream into the cooled egg mixture to lighten it, then fold the remaining cream and bananas into egg mixture.

Fill the pastry shells with banana cream and smooth to even.

Beat remaining cream until stiff.

Spoon around edge of the pies and sprinkle with chopped pecans, if desired.

Sausage & Peppers, Street Fair Style

1 lb Italian sausages, hot or sweet
3 lbs bell peppers
1 (35 ounce) can italian crushed tomatoes
1 clove garlic, crushed
1/2 teaspoon salt, to taste
pepper
1/8-1/4 teaspoon oregano
1/4 cup oil (I use olive oil)

Use a roasting pan large enough to hold all ingredients.

Clean peppers, cut into strips& place in the pan.

Cut sausage into 1 1/2 slices& put on top of the peppers.

Pour the tomatoes over them.

Sprinkle the oil and the rest of the ingredients over all.

Preheat oven to 375 degrees F.

Bake about an hour, stirring several times during the cooking. Serve in a dish or better yet, in sandwiches with crusty Italian bread or rolls.

All American County Fair Prize Winning Chili

1 can tomatoes
1 can tomato sauce
2 cans tomato paste
water
1 medium onion, chopped
3-5 cloves garlic, minced
4-5 stalks celery, chopped
1 green pepper, chopped
1 sweet red pepper, chopped
5 chili peppers, whole (cut slits lengthwise)
5 jalapeno peppers, whole (cut slits lengthwise)
1 zucchini, chopped
1 eggplant, chopped
1 bag baby carrots (whole)
mushrooms (whole)
1 bag frozen corn
steak, diced (any cut)
ground meat (any, I like to use chicken) dark red kidney beans, cooked
black turtle beans, cooked
lentils, cooked
1 pinch oregano
basil, to taste
1/4-1/2 teaspoon nutmeg
1/4 teaspoon cinnamon
black pepper
2 tablespoons cocoa powder

Put all ingrediants in a pot and cook for 5 to 10 hours.

Stir occasionally.

The ingredients list is enough to make 2 pots worth (dutch oven size). I usually omit the meat from one pot and make a vegetarian batch at the same time. It's good for your vegan friends and as lighter fare for lunch!

Put the chile and jalapeno peppers in last with their stems sticking up out of the chili. This makes them easy to remove for those who don't want their chili hot!

Candy-Coated Popcorn (Summer Fair Popcorn)

This is a sweet and tasty popcorn

3 tablespoons vegetable oil
1/3 cup popcorn (organic preferred)
3 tablespoons white sugar
salt (optional)

Heat oil in medium-sized pan over medium heat.

Add popcorn and sprinkle sugar over it.

Cover and shake continuously until popped.

For sweet and salty flavour, sprinkle with a little salt.

Carefully transfer to a bowl as melted, hot sugar can cause serious burns. Cool a few minutes before serving.

The End

www.ingramcontent.com/pod-product-compliance
Lightning Source LLC
Chambersburg PA
CBHW081417080526
44589CB00016B/2571